Tarot Card Notebooks

Made in United States
Troutdale, OR
07/15/2024

21254731R00070